P9-DCC-797

A GIFT FOR

⊰ FROM ⊱

100 Ways
to Keep Your Soul Alive

**Living Deeply and
Fully Every Day**

edited by
Frederic and Mary Ann Brussat

Hallmark
BOOKS

HarperSanFrancisco

PUBLISHED UNDER LICENSE FROM HARPERCOLLINS PUBLISHERS INC.

Book design by Ralph Fowler
Set in Stempel Schneidler
Illustrations by Kathleen Edwards

The Library of Congress has cataloged the original edition of this title as follows:

100 ways to keep your soul alive : living deeply and fully every day / edited by Frederic Brussat and Mary Ann Brussat.
    p. cm.
    Includes bibliographical references.
    ISBN 0–06–251050–9
    1. Spiritual life. 2. Soul. I. Brussat, Frederic. II. Brussat, Mary Ann. III. Title: One hundred ways to keep your soul alive. IV. Title: Hundred ways to keep your soul alive.

BL624.A17 1994
291.4'3—dc20   93–46210
                                                          CIP

ISBN 0-06-095390-X (Hallmark edition)

    00 01 02 03 RRD 10 9 8 7 6 5 4

Contents

Acknowledgments

This book emerged out of our reading and reviewing for *Values & Visions: A Resource Companion for Spiritual Journeys,* the membership magazine of Cultural Information Service (CIS), the nonprofit organization we founded and codirect. For their ongoing support of our explorations of spirituality and soul in the contemporary world, we are very grateful to all the members of CIS, especially Bill Moyers, Sam Keen, Howard Moody, Bryant Kirkland, Bill Malcomson, Philip Michael, Neil Topliffe, Jan and Cliff York, Marge and Paul Patterson, Karl Koss, Fred Hofheinz, Craig Dykstra, and Jim Wind. Special thanks to Carolyn Dutton, typist and fiddler extraordinaire, whose many gifts to us and CIS could never be properly summarized in a mere title.

We feel blessed to have shared our spiritual journeys with Patricia Repinski, Ieva Graufelds, Cora Louise Kevan, Les Schwartz, Debra Farrington, Kenyon Taylor, Lynn Nezin, and Joy Carol. Mary Ann has especially appreciated the friendship and guidance of Gerald Epstein as she has learned to understand the wondrous imagery of her inner life.

We want to thank all the writers represented in this book for their ideas and ideals. They have truly enriched our lives. Frederic salutes Thomas Moore for his watershed work on soul as he recalls with gratitude the epiphanies that accompanied his reading of *Care of the Soul*.

We value the many publishers and publicists who have cooperated with our efforts to keep on top of new books and who have introduced us to so many contemporary teachers. We are very pleased that Kandace Hawkinson, our editor at HarperSanFrancisco, recognized the wisdom in a collection of quotes published in *Values & Visions* and encouraged us to expand them for this book. We have enjoyed her insights and enthusiasm.

Finally, for their unique contributions to keeping our souls alive, our love to Boone and Bebb and Glory Days at Half Moon Bay.

Introduction

Keeping your soul alive is an adventure, a delightful challenge, a rousing responsibility, and an essential spiritual practice.

The phrase first leaped out at us from the pages of a 1990 novel, J. M. Coetzee's *Age of Iron*. The protagonist, a retired classics professor in South Africa, writes to her daughter: "I am trying to keep my soul alive in times not hospitable to soul." We decided to explore what that effort would require.

Keeping your soul alive, we soon learned, becomes urgent during tough times in your life. But it is perhaps even more crucial during good times. It is related to that process of coming into your own called "soulmaking"; it is about the kind of ongoing attention implied by the phrase "care of the soul."

What is required to keep your soul alive?

A detailed understanding of what "soul" means is not necessary. In fact, soul eludes explanation or location. It is not defined as much as it is recognized and expressed. We notice, for example, that some objects have "soul" and describe particular behaviors as "soulful."

Certain words are naturally attached to soul—words like *depth, meaning, value, essential nature, genuineness, imagination, passion, mystery.* We identify soul by the *quality* of our experiences.

Here are other indications of soul, along with some things we have come to understand as its messages.

✧ The soul savors the present moment. You don't find it hiding out in the past or waiting for you in the future. It says pay attention to what is happening to you right now.

✧ The soul speaks its own peculiar language in the messes and miseries of life. It does not run from trouble or lift itself above the fray of the everyday. Don't think you have to fix everything about yourself for your soul's sake.

✧ The soul savors simplicities—love that is true, wonder that is childlike, humility that is homegrown.

✧ The soul also revels in complexity. It is evident

in the maze of your feelings, thoughts, and commitments.

✧ The soul is a meaning maker, always putting odd combinations together and spawning new possibilities. It asks you to be open to the unusual and the new.

✧ The soul is deep and doesn't enjoy skimming the surface. It locates treasures by getting to the bottom of things.

✧ The soul is always on the lookout for fresh wonders. It likes taking the long way home. Be patient with its haphazard and zigzag meanderings.

✧ The soul cherishes pleasure. It delights in the senses and the luxuries of leisure time. It wants you to indulge yourself occasionally.

✧ The soul yearns for beauty and will seek it out continually. It invites you to join the quest.

✧ The soul and joy are good friends. Let them be together as often as possible. Always give the soul's ardors full expression. Don't suppress your enthusiasm and your ecstasy—or your tears.

✧ The soul reaches out to others through love, compassion, and forgiveness. Let its music play through your words and deeds.

✧ The soul satisfies itself and finds fulfillment in community. Recognize that your family, friends, neighbors, and colleagues all represent opportunities for spiritual collaboration.

✧ The soul's embrace of people and things is wide and welcoming. It is hospitable to strangers and revels in the opportunity to be an angel for another soul in need. Never constrain this impulse.

✧ The soul expresses itself through image and imagination. It is a great storyteller spinning yarns in your dreams and fantasies. Don't ignore these messages.

✧ The soul stretches itself through risk, renewal, and travel. Don't be afraid; be adventurous.

✧ The soul seeks out silence and solitude in order to hear the soft voice of God. Treasure the quiet times and make a place for them in your busy life.

✧ The soul is fed by lifelong learning. Many sacred texts and other resources will speak to your deepest needs and illuminate your path. Remember that a little study every day is good for the soul.

✧ The soul is nourished by ritual and celebration. Punctuate your life with these special occasions.

✧ The soul gives thanks and counts blessings. Notice this activity. The soul knows we usually have more than we need or deserve.

✧ The soul itself is a mystery and therefore has great respect for the inexplicable. Don't try to figure everything out.

We skate around an explanation of soul and end up with these indications and imperatives. What we know is that we dare not ignore this essential dimension of our lives. The more we try to understand it, the more we are convinced of the importance of honoring, nurturing, healing, stretching, and caring for our souls.

Throughout the ages, spiritual teachers, mystics, philosophers, activists, and artists have shown us that there are specific ways to keep our souls alive. This book includes one hundred of their suggestions. Here are places to be, attitudes to assume, perspectives to embrace, actions to try.

Some of these strategies are from ancient teachers and texts, but most are from contemporary writers. We urge you to explore their works and discover even more ways to keep your soul alive.

The quotations are followed by invitations to do something practical and specific. Think of these as good first steps for keeping your soul alive. Like many first steps, some of them are questions.

This book does not present a self-improvement program for problem-free living. Soul is not about satisfaction, comfort, or entertainment. Follow the advice given here and most likely you will find yourself more connected not only to your inner life but also to your neighbors and the larger world. Such soulful connections are rarely without pain and complexity, but they are marks of a deep and full life.

This collection of quotations and activities does not try to pinpoint the "right" ways or the only steps to keep your soul alive. Look closely and you'll see that some strategies actually contradict others.

You are bound to have some favorites. We certainly do. But what will soon be clear is that there is no one way to soul that is appropriate for every individual at every time.

About soul, we can never be definitive. Keeping your soul alive is not about doing either this or that. Soul is always both this and . . .

1

Live in This Moment

I was regretting the past and fearing the future. Suddenly God was speaking. "My name is 'I Am.'" I waited. God continued.

"When you live in the past, with its mistakes and regrets, it is hard. I am not there. My name is not 'I was.'

"When you live in the future, with its problems and fears, it is hard. I am not there. My name is not 'I will be.'

"When you live in this moment, it is not hard. I am here. My name is 'I Am.'"

—HELEN MELLICOST
  quoted in *One Hundred Graces*

Do something completely on the spur of the moment today, without thinking about past experiences or future consequences.

2

Go into All Four Rooms

There is an Indian proverb or axiom that says that everyone is a house with four rooms, a physical, a mental, an emotional, and a spiritual. Most of us tend to live in one room most of the time but, unless we go into every room every day, even if only to keep it aired, we are not a complete person.

—RUMER GODDEN
in *A House with Four Rooms*

Assess the condition of your four rooms.
Which one looks like you visit it regularly?
Which needs airing out?

3

Be Kind

We cannot make the Kingdom of God happen, but we can put out leaves as it draws near. We can be kind to each other. We can be kind to ourselves. We can drive back the darkness a little. We can make green places within ourselves and among ourselves where God can make his Kingdom happen.

—FREDERICK BUECHNER
in *The Clown in the Belfry*

*Give yourself and a
friend bouquets of fresh flowers.*

4

Try Not to Panic

I will try not to panic, to keep my standard of living modest and to work steadily, even shyly, in the spirit of those medieval carvers who so fondly sculpted the undersides of choir seats.

—JOHN UPDIKE
   quoted in *Life* magazine

*Act today without
expecting to receive any recognition
or reward in return.*

5

Pay Attention

The "burning bush" was not a miracle. It was a test. God wanted to find out whether or not Moses could pay attention to something for more than a few minutes. When Moses did, God spoke. The trick is to pay attention to what is going on around you long enough to behold the miracle without falling asleep. There is another world, right here within this one, whenever we pay attention.

—LAWRENCE KUSHNER
in *God Was in This Place and I,*
i Did Not Know

Stop what you are doing
and observe your surroundings.
Keep watching until you
notice a miracle.

6

Seek the Sacred
in the Ordinary

The great lesson from the true mystics . . . is that
the sacred is *in* the ordinary, that it is to be found in
one's daily life, in one's neighbors, friends, and
family, in one's backyard. . . .

—ABRAHAM H. MASLOW
in *Religions, Values, and
Peak-Experiences*

*Find evidence of the sacred
in your garden, on your street, or in your neighborhood.
What about this ordinary
place is extraordinary?*

Discover the Soul in Things

Living artfully might require taking the time to buy things with soul for the home. Good linens, a special rug, or a simple teapot can be a source of enrichment not only in our own life, but also in the lives of our children and grandchildren. The soul basks in this extended sense of time. But we can't discover the soul in a thing without first taking time to observe it and be with it for a while. This kind of observation has a quality of intimacy about it.

—THOMAS MOORE
in *Care of the Soul*

*Buy, find, or create an object
for your home that you would like
future generations to cherish.*

8

Fan the Light

Invite the Sacred to participate in your joy in little things, as well as in your agony over the great ones. There are as many miracles to be seen through a microscope as through a telescope. Start with little things seen through the magnifying glass of wonder, and just as a magnifying glass can focus the sunlight into a burning beam that can set a leaf aflame, so can your focused wonder set you ablaze with insight. Find the light in each other and just fan it.

—ALICE O. HOWELL
in *The Dove in the Stone*

---

*Identify one little thing
about another person that amazes
you and encourage it.*

Keep Your Flowerness Alive

All of us, children and adults, are beautiful flowers. Our eyelids are exactly like rose petals, especially when our eyes are closed. Our ears are like morning glories listening to the sounds of birds. Our lips form a beautiful flower every time we smile. And our two hands are a lotus flower with five petals. The practice is to keep our "flowerness" alive and present, not just for our own benefit but for the happiness of everyone.

—THICH NHAT HANH
in *Touching Peace*

*Notice how you connect
with the world through your eyes,
ears, lips, and hands.*

10

Distinguish the Dawn

An old rabbi once asked his pupils how they could tell when the night had ended and the day had begun.

"Could it be," asked one of the students, "when you can see an animal in the distance and tell whether it's a sheep or a dog?"

"No," answered the rabbi.

Another asked, "Is it when you can look at a tree in the distance and tell whether it's a fig tree or a peach tree?"

"No," answered the rabbi.

"Then when is it?" the pupils demanded.

"It is when you can look on the face of any man or woman and see that it is your sister or brother. Because if you cannot see this, it is still night."

—HASIDIC TALE
quoted in *Peacemaking Day by Day*

Look through a book of photographs from around the world. Address the people pictured there as "brother" and "sister."

Live in a Large Moral House

I am personally thankful that we live together in a large moral house even if we do not drink at the same fountain of faith. The world we experience together is one world, God's world, and our world, and the problems we share are common human problems. So we can talk together, try to understand each other, and help each other.

—LEWIS B. SMEDES
in *Choices*

*Recount one insight about
yourself or the world that you gained
through meeting someone from
another culture.*

12

Mend the World

Mending is a good metaphor for daily spiritual life. We are each part of the great woven fabric of the world community. When a couple in their mud brick house in Africa maintains a just and joyful relationship, the world is a little bit better place because of them. . . . We are valuable members of the human community when we take our own moral inventory and make daily repairs for our mistakes.

—MAVIS AND MERLE FOSSOM
in *The More We Find in Each Other*

*Review your actions during the
past twenty-four hours. Imagine yourself
correcting all your mistakes, and act on one
correction before going to sleep.*

Pray for Somebody

I remember reading years ago a little tract written by Frank Laubach, a great man of prayer, in which he described one of his prayer practices. When he is on a journey, even on a streetcar going a few blocks, he tries to spot somebody on the car who seems to him to be in distress, or perhaps just tired or lonely, and to direct his prayers toward that person as though the Divine possession were streaming out from him to this other person.

—H. L. PUXLEY
in *International Journal of Parapsychology*

*The next time you are on a
subway or a bus, at the movies or
in the mall, choose someone in need
and pray for that person.*

14

Seek Essential Wealth

What is most necessary for man and what is given him in great abundance, are experiences, especially experiences of the forces within him. This is his most essential food, his most essential wealth. If man consciously receives all this abundance, the universe will pour into him what is called *life* in Judaism, *spirit* in Christianity, *light* in Islam, *power* in Taoism.

—JACOB NEEDLEMAN
in *Money and the Meaning of Life*

Name one treasure within yourself. How do you experience its abundance?

15

Be Spiritually Inebriated

Spiritual inebriation is this: that a man receives more sensible joy and sweetness than his heart can either contain or desire. Spiritual inebriation brings forth many strange gestures in men. It makes some sing and praise God because of their fulness of joy, and some weep with great tears because of their sweetness of heart. It makes one restless in all his limbs, so that he must run and jump and dance; and so excites another that he must gesticulate and clap his hands.

—JOHN OF RUYSBROECK
quoted in *The Common Experience*

Exaggerate a behavior to show that there are times when you just can't contain yourself.

16

Have a Beginner's Mind

If your mind is empty, it is always ready for anything; it is open to everything. In the beginner's mind there are many possibilities, in the expert's mind there are few.

—SHUNRYU SUZUKI-ROSHI
in *Zen Mind, Beginner's Mind*

*Identify one area in
which you are truly a beginner.*

17

Be Open to Epiphanies

An epiphany is a sudden realization of a significant truth, usually arising out of a commonplace event. At that special moment, a life meaning becomes clear to you—an insight into your personality, a discovery of something you value or believe in, an acute sense of where you are in life. . . . Such moments can determine the course of your life as much as your response to a crisis.

—ROBERT U. AKERET
with DANIEL KLEIN
in *Family Tales, Family Wisdom*

*Share with a friend one
epiphany you have had. How did
it change your life?*

Don't Live Superficially

You know of the disease in Central Africa called sleeping sickness. . . . There also exists a sleeping sickness of the soul. Its most dangerous aspect is that one is unaware of its coming. That is why you have to be careful. As soon as you notice the slightest sign of indifference, the moment you become aware of the loss of a certain seriousness, of longing, of enthusiasm and zest, take it as a warning. You should realize your soul suffers if you live superficially.

—ALBERT SCHWEITZER
quoted in *The Search for Meaning*

*Watch your reactions to people
and events today. Do you tend to be
indifferent or enthusiastic?*

19

Go on a Spiritual Retreat

A spiritual retreat is medicine for soul starvation. Through silence, solitary practice, and simple living, we begin to fill the empty reservoir. This lifts the veils, dissolves the masks, and creates space within for the feelings of forgiveness, compassion, and loving kindness that are so often blocked.

—DAVID A. COOPER
in *Silence, Simplicity, and Solitude*

*Plan a retreat from your
normal activities, even if you can get
away only for a few hours.*

Be Compassionate

Compassion is the basis of all truthful relationship: it means being present with love—for ourselves and for all life, including animals, fish, birds, and trees. Compassion is bringing our deepest truth into our actions, no matter how much the world seems to resist, because that is ultimately what we have to give this world and one another.

—RAM DASS
in *Compassion in Action*

*Who and what needs
your compassion today?*

21

Cultivate Justice

Justice is a complex set of passions to be cultivated, not an abstract set of principles to be formulated, mastered, and imposed upon society.... Our knowledge of justice begins with our experience of our own place in the world; our sense of justice is first of all our emotional response to a world that does not always meet up with our expectations and demands. Our sense of justice, in other words, has its origins in such emotions as resentment, jealousy, outrage, and revenge as well as in care and compassion.

—ROBERT C. SOLOMON
in *A Passion for Justice*

Name an injustice that troubles you. What emotion first made you aware of it?

Don't Let the World Define You

A little criticism makes me angry, and a little rejection makes me depressed. A little praise raises my spirits, and a little success excites me. It takes very little to raise me up or thrust me down. Often I am like a small boat on the ocean, completely at the mercy of its waves. All the time and energy I spend in keeping some kind of balance and preventing myself from being tipped over and drowning shows my life is mostly a struggle for survival: not a holy struggle, but an anxious struggle resulting from the mistaken idea that it is the world that defines me.

—HENRI J. M. NOUWEN
in *The Return of the Prodigal Son*

*Make a list of the
things others say about you
and then rip it up.*

23

Be Hospitable

Hospitality means we take people into the space that is our lives and our minds and our hearts and our work and our efforts. Hospitality is the way we come out of ourselves. It is the first step toward dismantling the barriers of the world. Hospitality is the way we turn a prejudiced world around, one heart at a time.

—JOAN D. CHITTISTER, O.S.B.
in *Wisdom Distilled from the Daily*

*Show hospitality to one
person today—with an open door,
an invitation, or a look.*

Love the Leper Within

God calls all of you to take the path of the inner truth—and that means taking responsibility for *everything* that's in you: for what pleases you and for what you're ashamed of, for the rich person inside you and for the poor one. Francis of Assisi called this, "loving the leper within us." If you learn to love the poor one within you, you'll discover that you have room to have compassion "outside" too, that there's room in you for others, for those who are different from you, for the least among your brothers and sisters.

—RICHARD ROHR
 in *Simplicity*

Write a friendly dialogue between
yourself and that part of yourself of
which you are ashamed.

Don't Make Comparisons

Everybody is unique.
Compare not yourself with anybody else
lest you spoil God's curriculum.

—BAAL SHEM TOV

*Create a self-portrait—a drawing,
clay model, or collage—that illustrates
what is unique about you.*

Know When Enough Is Enough

Great trouble comes
From not knowing what is enough.
Great conflict arises from wanting too much.
When we know when enough is enough,
There will always be enough.
(Tao 46)

—LAO TZU
  quoted in *The Tao of Peace*

*Compile a list of excesses in
your life—possessions, behaviors, ideas.
Which could you do without?*

Repair Your Karma

Karma Repair Kit: Items 1–4

1. Get enough food to eat, and eat it.
2. Find a place to sleep where it is quiet, and sleep there.
3. Reduce intellectual and emotional noise until you arrive at the silence of yourself, and listen to it.
4.

    —RICHARD BRAUTIGAN
      in *The Pill Versus the Springhill Mine Disaster*

*For the next few hours,
notice what distracts your attention
from what you are doing.*

Fit a Place

When we enter the landscape to learn something, we are obligated, I think, to pay attention rather than constantly to pose questions. To approach the land as we would a person, by opening an intelligent conversation. And to stay in one place, to make of that one, long observation a fully dilated experience. We will always be rewarded if we give the land credit for more than we imagine, and if we imagine it as being more complex even than language. In these ways we begin, I think, to find a home, to sense how to fit a place.

—BARRY LOPEZ
in *The Rediscovery of
North America*

*Take a walk around the place
where you live. What complexities
about it do you observe?*

Exercise Your Imagination

Imagination has the creative task of making symbols, joining things together in such a way that they throw new light on each other and on everything around them. The imagination is a discovering faculty, a faculty for seeing relationships, for seeing meanings that are special and even quite new.

—THOMAS MERTON
in *Contemplation in a
World of Action*

———

*Look around and focus on two objects
or people. Using your imagination, establish
a relationship between the two.*

Open Yourself to Imagery

You, like every human being, are a storyteller by birthright. You are born with an endless supply of personal and universal themes. It is important to open yourself to receive the vast wealth of imagery that lives within you. Build a hearth within you and let it become a circle of protection. In it your heart's wisdom may ignite and burn. Ask that all who gather at your fire from your own inner skies, lands, and waters come with goodwill to share their truths in its warmth.

—NANCY MELLON
    in *Storytelling & the
    Art of Imagination*

*Close your eyes and see yourself
telling a story. What is it about?
Who is listening?*

Act Out Your Dreams

Great dreams contain inexhaustible truths, and orient us, like runes, toward our futures. One hesitates to try to explain them; one wants to dance them, act them out in living gestures. The more we put ourselves into a great dream, the more we get back. Great dreams are wells that never run dry.

—MICHAEL GROSSO
in *Soulmaker*

*Follow through on something
started in one of your night dreams—
call someone you met in the dream
or visit a place seen there.*

See Unwrapped Gifts and Surprises

When I was six or seven years old, growing up in Pittsburgh, I used to take a precious penny of my own and hide it for someone else to find. I was greatly excited . . . at the thought of the first lucky passerby who would receive in this way, regardless of merit, a free gift from the universe. . . .

I've been thinking about seeing. There are lots of things to see, unwrapped gifts and free surprises. The world is fairly studded and strewn with pennies cast broadside from a generous hand.

—ANNIE DILLARD
  in *Pilgrim at Tinker Creek*

*Think of three ways
you can recapture the wonder
you had as a child.*

Share the Beauty

We all share beauty. It strikes us indiscriminately.
. . . There is no end to beauty for the person who is
aware. Even the cracks between the sidewalk contain geometric patterns of amazing beauty. If we
take pictures of them and blow up the photographs,
we realize we walk on beauty every day, even
when things seem ugly around us.

—MATTHEW FOX
in *Creation Spirituality*

Describe the most
surprisingly beautiful thing
you have seen today.

Learn Something New

When I learn something new—and it happens every day—I feel a little more at home in the universe, a little more comfortable in the nest.

—BILL MOYERS
   in *A World of Ideas*

Watch a TV program, read an article, or attend a lecture on a subject you know nothing about.

Think Positively

Traveler: What kind of weather are we going to have today?

Shepherd: The kind of weather I like.

Traveler: How do you know it will be the kind of weather you like?

Shepherd: Having found out, sir, I cannot always get what I like, I have learned always to like what I get. So I am quite sure we will have the kind of weather I like.

—ANTHONY DE MELLO, S.J.
in *The Heart of the Enlightened*

Evaluate your attitudes toward those things, like the weather, that you cannot control. Are you usually negative or positive?

Get the Piñata Perspective

See, the human mind is kind of like . . .
a piñata. When it breaks open,
there's a lot of surprises inside.
Once you get the piñata perspective,
you see that losing your mind
can be a peak experience.

—JANE WAGNER
in *The Search for Signs of
Intelligent Life in the Universe*

*Do something completely
outrageous today.*

Shed an Old Skin

We must be willing to get rid of
the life we've planned, so as to have
the life that is waiting for us.

The old skin has to be shed
before the new one can come.

—JOSEPH CAMPBELL
in *A Joseph Campbell Companion*

*Drop a habit that has kept you
from reaching your potential.*

Do Nothing

A carpenter and his apprentice were walking together through a large forest. And when they came across a tall, huge, gnarled, old, beautiful oak tree, the carpenter asked his apprentice: "Do you know why this tree is so tall, so huge, so gnarled, so old and beautiful?" The apprentice looked at his master and said: "No . . . why?" "Well," the carpenter said, "because it is useless. If it had been useful it would have been cut long ago and made into tables and chairs, but because it is useless it could grow so tall and so beautiful that you can sit in its shade and relax."

—TAO STORY
in *The Blessings of Imperfection*

Try just being for an hour.
Don't worry about whether you are
productive or effective.

Don't Try to See Through the Distances

Keep walking, though there's no place to get to.
Don't try to see through the distances.
That's not for human beings. Move within,
but don't move the way fear makes you move.

—RUMI
in *Unseen Rain,*
Quatrains of Rumi

Stop reading all those
predictions about the future that you
find in newspapers and books.

Accept Uncertainty as a Blessing

Life is. I am. Anything might happen.

And I believe I *may* invest my life with meaning.

The uncertainty is a blessing in disguise.

If I were absolutely certain about all things, I would spend my life in anxious misery, fearful of losing my way. But since everything and anything are always possible, the miraculous is always nearby and wonders shall never, ever cease.

—ROBERT FULGHUM
   in *Maybe (Maybe Not)*

*The next time you find
yourself asking why and how and
when, don't answer.*

Read the Signs

I suspect we are all recipients of cosmic love notes. Messages, omens, voices, cries, revelations, and appeals are homogenized into each day's events. If only we knew how to listen, to read the signs.

—SAM KEEN
in *The Passionate Life*

Watch for a sign today—two
events that you might call coincidences or
an unsolicited confirmation of what you have
been thinking. What's the message?

Be Playful

A buoyant and full-blooded soul has quick senses and miscellaneous sympathies: it changes with the changing world; and when not too much starved or thwarted by circumstances, it finds all things vivid and comic. Life is free play fundamentally and would like to be free play altogether.

—GEORGE SANTAYANA
in *Soliloquies in England
and Later Soliloquies*

*Take an afternoon off and go
to the park. Play on the equipment
you most enjoyed as a child.*

Do Rituals

Rituals are a central part of life whether it be in how meals are shared together, or how major events are marked. . . . Rituals give us places to be playful, to explore the meaning of our lives, and to rework and rebuild family relationships. They connect us with our past, define our present life, and show us a path to our future as we pass on ceremonies, traditions, objects, symbols, and ways of being with each other, handed down from previous generations.

—EVAN IMBER-BLACK
and JANINE ROBERTS
in *Rituals for Our Times*

*Name the one ritual—religious,
family, or personal—that means the most to
you. Why is it so significant?*

44

Live a Measured Life

Peace comes from living a measured life. Peace comes from attending to every part of my world in a sacramental way. My relationships are not what I do when I have time left over from my work. . . . Reading is not something I do when life calms down. Prayer is not something I do when I feel like it. They are all channels of hope and growth for me. They must all be given their due.

—JOAN D. CHITTISTER, O.S.B.
in *Wisdom Distilled from the Daily*

*For one day, keep track of your
activities and the approximate time you
give them. What adjustments could you make
to use your time more soulfully?*

Sing a Song of Goodness

In his collection of Bengali poems, *Gitanjali*, Rabindranath Tagore writes that the song he wanted to sing has never happened because he spent his days "stringing and unstringing" his instrument. Whenever I read these lines a certain sadness enters my soul. . . . I get so preoccupied with the details and pressure of my schedule, with the hurry and worry of life, that I miss the song of goodness which is waiting to be sung through me.

—JOYCE RUPP
in *May I Have This Dance?*

*Give up one activity
that blocks you from getting on
with the joy of living.*

Let Your Tears Flow

That tears have a purifying, rejuvenating, and light-bearing power and capability—this was known by the Masters of spiritual life; the hermits, monks, and members of spiritual orders in the past. The "gift of tears" was highly esteemed by them. . . . And just as the moving waters precede the appearance of the rainbow in the primeval light, so does weeping precede the rainbow of illuminating light in the soul.

—VALENTIN TOMBERG
in *Covenant of the Heart*

*Rent a movie that has
moved you to tears. Cry freely
as you watch it again.*

Put Love into the World

The roots of love sink down and deep and strike out far, and they are arteries that feed our lives, so we must see that they get the water and sun they need so they can nourish us. And when you put something good into the world, something good comes back to you.

—MERLE SHAIN
in *Hearts That We
Broke Long Ago*

*Recall a time when you felt
nourished by the love of others.*

48

Enjoy the World

Your enjoyment of the world is never right, till every Morning you wake in Heaven; see yourself in your Father's Palace; and look upon the Skies, the Earth and the Air as Celestial Joys: having such a Reverend Esteem of all, as if you were among the Angels.

—THOMAS TRAHERNE
quoted in *Enjoying the World*

*Pretend you are a traveler in
the Kingdom of Enjoyment. What old
or new places would you visit?*

Don't Focus on What You Don't Have

There's only one reason why you're not experiencing bliss at this present moment, and it's because you're thinking or focusing on what you don't have. . . . Right now you have everything you need to be in bliss.

Jesus was talking horse sense to lay people, to starving people, to poor people. He was telling them good news: It's yours for the taking.

—ANTHONY DE MELLO, S.J.
in *Awareness*

*Count your blessings today.
What would it take to convince you
that you already have it all?*

Live in Awe

Awe enables us to perceive in the world intimations of the divine, to sense in small things the beginning of infinite significance, to sense the ultimate in the common and the simple; to feel in the rush of the passing the stillness of the eternal.

—ABRAHAM JOSHUA HESCHEL
in *The Wisdom of Heschel*

*What intimations or hints
of God have you felt recently
in your daily life?*

Give Your Unique Gift

Each of us, as we journey through life, has the opportunity to find and to give his or her unique gift. Whether this gift is quiet or small in the eyes of the world does not matter at all—not at all; it is through the finding and the giving that we may come to know the joy that lies at the center of both the dark times and the light.

—HELEN M. LUKE
   in *Kaleidoscope*

Identify one talent you possess
that has enriched the lives of others.

Just Do It

The young salesman approached the farmer and began to talk excitedly about the book he was carrying. "This book will tell you everything you need to know about farming," the young man said enthusiastically. "It tells you when to sow and when to reap. It tells you about weather, what to expect and when to expect it. This book tells you all you need to know."

"Young man," the farmer said, "that's not the problem. I know everything that is in that book. My problem is doing it."

—JOSEPH GOSSE
   in *Spiritual Life* magazine

---

*Consider one project you are
having trouble finishing. What is the
first thing you need to do on it?*

53

Be Creative

Creativity belongs to the artist in each of us. To create means to relate. The root meaning of the word *art* is *to fit together* and we all do this every day. . . . Each time we fit things together we are creating—whether it is to make a loaf of bread, a child, a day.

—CORITA KENT
and JAN STEWARD
in *Learning by Heart*

With pen, paints, crayons, newspaper clippings, photographs, and household items, create a collage that reflects some of the things you would like to fit together.

Know What Time It Is

The wise man knows what time it is in his own life and in the life of the community. He knows that sensing the *kairos* (the prepared or ripe moment) is more important than conforming to the compulsive rhythm of chronological time. Thus, the wise man is able to give himself gracefully to seemingly contradictory experiences, because he knows that they belong to different seasons of life, all of which are necessary to the whole. Spring and winter, growth and decay, creativity and fallowness, health and sickness, power and impotence, and life and death all belong within the economy of being.

—SAM KEEN
   in *Apology for Wonder*

*In your life, is it time for
growth or pulling back, for hard
work or relaxation?*

Catch the Moment of Grace

The moment of grace comes to us *in* the dynamics of any situation we walk into. It is an opportunity that God sews into the fabric of a routine situation. It is a chance to do something creative, something helpful, something healing, something that makes one unmarked spot in the world better off for our having been there. We catch it if we are people of discernment.

—LEWIS B. SMEDES
in *A Pretty Good Person*

---

*Describe an incident when
you were in the right place at the
right time and the world was a better
place because of what you did.*

Read a Book

In real life I have qualms, a moral code, a sense of duty. I live within confines. In books, I am free to soar and to explore. There are no limits to my being.

Books, with their secret knowledge, free me from myself. I'm never alone. The greatest minds in history wait by my bed, sit patiently in bookcases, respond to my touch. I reach out and they are there, waiting to transport me to another realm.

—LINDA WELTNER
    in *No Place Like Home*

*Take a whole day off from your
regular activities and spend it with a book
you have always wanted to read.*

Dive for Ancient Wisdom

The religious searcher should be a diver through the deeps of ancient wisdom, seeking to bring up to the surface those concepts that can illuminate life today. Not all truth will be discovered in what is to come; some must be recalled from what has been forgotten.

—DAVID J. WOLPE
in *In Speech and in Silence*

---

*Study a sacred text—the Bible,
the Koran, the Tao Te Ching, or another—
and find one concept that stirs your soul.*

Keep the Sabbath

The Sabbath is more than an armistice, more than an interlude; it is a profound conscious harmony of man and the world, a sympathy for all things and a participation in the spirit that unites what is below and what is above. All that is divine in the world is brought into union with God. This is Sabbath, and the true happiness of the universe.

—ABRAHAM JOSHUA HESCHEL
in *The Sabbath*

*Rest for one day this week. Try
not to do any of the things you usually do.
Instead, tune into the larger world.*

Hold Death Close

Death is by no means separate from life. . . . We all interact with death every day, tasting it as we might a wine, feeling its keen edge even in trifling losses and disappointments, holding it by the hand, as a dancer might a partner, in every separation. We pump the soul into every mystery from within, from inside our own experience.

—EUGENE KENNEDY
in *On Being a Friend*

*Think about the little deaths you
have experienced during the past week.
What was your soul trying to tell you?*

Honor Your Ancestors

We inherit from our ancestors gifts so often taken for granted—our names, the color of our eyes and the texture of our hair, the unfolding of varied abilities and interests in different subjects, . . .

Each of us contains within our fragile vessels of skin and bones and cells this inheritance of soul. We are links between the ages, containing past and present expectations, sacred memories and future promise. Only when we recognize that we are heirs can we truly be pioneers.

—EDWARD C. SELLNER
in *Mentoring*

*Contemplate how your ancestors
live in you. What talents and interests
have you inherited?*

Sense Future Generations

Just as the life that pulses in our bodies goes back to the beginnings of the Earth, so too does that heartbeat carry the pulse of those that come after. By the power of our imagination we can sense the future generations breathing with the rhythm of our own breath or feel them hovering like a cloud of witnesses. Sometimes I fancy that if I were to turn my head suddenly, I would glimpse them over my shoulder. They and their claim to life have become that real to me.

—JOANNA MACY
in *The Way Ahead*

Imagine you are surrounded by
your descendants and future generations.
What do they need from you?

Be a Transformer

We're all assigned a piece of garden, a corner of the universe that is ours to transform. Our corner of the universe is our own life—our relationships, our homes, our work, our current circumstances—exactly as they are. Every situation we find ourselves in is an opportunity, perfectly planned by the Holy Spirit, to teach love instead of fear.

—MARIANNE WILLIAMSON
in *A Return to Love*

*Name one thing
that is within your power to
change and change it.*

Don't Miss the Party

God is spreading grace around in the world like a five-year-old spreads peanut butter; thickly, sloppily, eagerly, and if we are in the back shed trying to stay clean, we won't even get a taste.

—DONNA SCHAPER
in *Stripping Down*

*Throw caution to
the wind and jump into the
midst of things today.*

Recognize Magic

Magic is a sudden opening of the mind to the wonder of existence. It is a sense that there is much more to life than we usually recognize; that we do not have to be confined by the limited views that our family, our society, or our own habitual thoughts impose on us; that life contains many dimensions, depths, textures, and meanings extending far beyond our familiar beliefs and concepts.

—JOHN WELWOOD
in *Ordinary Magic*

*Recall a moment in your life
that felt like magic—perhaps the first
time you met a special person or a
surprising turn of events.*

Use Your Senses

William Blake says the body is "that portion of Soul discerned by the five Senses." I live with that idea. I sit and look out my window here in Canada and the autumn trees are golden against the blue sky. I can feel their "food" coming into my eyes and going down, down, down, interacting inside, and I fill up with gold. My soul is fed. I see, I smell, I taste, I hear, I touch. Through the orifices of my body, I give and I receive. I am not trying to capture what is absent. It's that interchange between the embodied soul and the outside world that is the dynamic process. That's how growth takes place. That is life.

—MARION WOODMAN
   in *Conscious Femininity*

Pay attention to your senses today.
What do they have to report?

Learn from Your Body

My body has taught me many things, all of them filled with soul: how to dance and make love, mourn and make music; now it is teaching me how to heal. I am learning to heed the shifting currents of my body—the subtle changes in temperature, muscle tension, thought and mood—the way a sailor rides the wind by reading the ripples on the water.

—KAT DUFF
in *The Alchemy of Illness*

*List three things you have
learned from your body recently.*

Embrace Emptiness

Healthy mysticism praises acts of letting go, of being emptied, of getting in touch with the space inside and expanding this until it merges with the space outside. Space meeting space; empty pouring into empty. Births happen from that encounter with emptiness, nothingness.... Let us not fight emptiness and nothingness, but allow it to penetrate us even as we penetrate it.

—MATTHEW FOX
in *Creation Spirituality*

*Let go of an idea, a belief, an
explanation, or a relationship that you
have used to prop up your life.*

Travel

Often I feel I go to some distant region of the world to be reminded of who I really am. There is no mystery about why this should be so. Stripped of your ordinary surroundings, your friends, your daily routines, . . . you are forced into direct experience. Such direct experience inevitably makes you aware of who it is that is having the experience. That's not always comfortable, but it is always invigorating.

—MICHAEL CRICHTON
in *Travels*

*Look at photographs taken
during a trip. What did you find out
about yourself on this journey?*

Love a Place

An act of love or giving is the single most powerful act in making or using a place. . . . The most mundane building can be transformed through the spirit with which it is used, expressed in the flowers in the window, the well-scrubbed doorstep, or the smell of freshly baked bread. What counts is that someone has done the best, not the least, they could. And that comes not from necessity, but only from love.

—THOMAS BENDER
   in *The Power of Place*

Write a love letter to the place where you live. Sing its praises in specifics.

70

Let Stories Happen to You

I hope you will go out and let stories happen to you, and that you will work them, water them with your blood and tears and your laughter till they bloom, till you yourself burst into bloom.

—CLARISSA PINKOLA ESTÉS
in *Women Who Run with the Wolves*

---

*Choose one story about a person
in your family and turn it over in your
mind until you discover how it has brought
laughter or tears into your life.*

Practice Daily Arts

As we practice our daily arts, if only in the composing of a heart-felt letter, we are unearthing the eternal from within ordinary time, engaging in the special qualities, themes, and circumstances of the soul. Soul thrives as we jot down a thought in our diary or note a dream, and give body to a slight influx of eternity. Our notebooks then truly become our own private gospels and sutras, our holy books, and our simple paintings truly serve as icons, every bit as significant in the work of our own soul as the wonderful icons of the Eastern churches are for their congregations.

—THOMAS MOORE
in *Care of the Soul*

---

*Make your own holy book using excerpts
from your journal, drawings, letters, favorite
photographs, poetry, and quotations.*

Find Your Vocation

What you need to do is think of work as "vocation." This word may seem stilted in its tone, but it has a wisdom within it. It comes from the Latin word for calling, which comes from the word for voice. In those meanings it touches on what work really should be. It should be something that calls to you as something you want to do, and it should be something that gives voice to who you are and what you want to say to the world.

—KENT NERBURN
in *Letters to My Son*

---

*Pin down the two things you like
best about your work. Reflect upon how these activities
are expressions of your soul.*

Hear Your Inner Voice

My dad always used to say, "If you take a step and it feels good, you must be headed in the right direction." What he wanted us to understand was that we needed to measure our progress against an inner compass, using our feelings, our comfort level, and our knowledge of ourselves as the ultimate guide. . . .

I've spent most of my adult life trying to hear that inner voice above the noise around me. . . . It says softly that happiness is as simple as having something to look forward to in the morning. . . . It says, in a low murmur I sometimes have to strain to hear, that now is the time to have fun.

—LINDA WELTNER
in *No Place Like Home*

*Think about the last time
you listened to your inner voice.
What did it say?*

Indulge Yourself

Pleasing yourself with special treats from time to time is vital to a healthy, satisfying life. . . . We need to surround ourselves with little rewards that mean something to us, that we can keep separate. Whether it be a sip of wine, a shopping spree, a well-deserved vacation, a vigorous laugh, or a satisfying cry—such small indulgences can brighten and enliven our lives.

—ROBERT ORNSTEIN
and DAVID SOBEL
in *Healthy Pleasures*

*Treat yourself to something special
you've desired for a long time.*

Look for Contemporaries

"Who are my contemporaries?" Juan Gelman asks himself.

Juan says that sometimes he comes across men who smell of fear, in Buenos Aires, Paris, or anywhere in the world, and feels that these men are not his contemporaries. But there is a Chinese who, thousands of years ago, wrote a poem about a goatherd who is far from his beloved, and yet can hear in the middle of the night, in the middle of the snow, the sound of her comb running through her hair. And reading this distant poem, Juan finds that yes, these people—the poet, the goatherd and the woman—are truly his contemporaries.

—EDUARDO GALEANO
in *The Book of Embraces*

Send a note of appreciation to someone who shares your enthusiasms and always seems to be on the same wavelength.

Acknowledge the Angels

Every blade of grass has an angel that bends over it and whispers, "Grow! Grow!"

—THE TALMUD
quoted in *Storytelling &
the Art of Imagination*

---

*Wing a prayer to the angel who
has brought you through difficult times
or blessed you with unexpected joy.*

Believe in Prophets

Never, ever, regret or apologize for believing that when one man or one woman decides to risk addressing the world with truth, the world may stop what it is doing and hear.

There is too much evidence to the contrary. . . .

The myth of the impossible dream is more powerful than all the facts of history.

—ROBERT FULGHUM
   in *Maybe (Maybe Not)*

Show your solidarity with someone who
is trying to right a wrong and change the world.
Send a contribution or volunteer your services.

Watch for Saints

It is not so much a question of where to look to find saints, rather it is merely the need to remove the blinders from our eyes, for saints are here in our age just as they have been for every age for the past two millennia.

—JOHN J. DELANEY
   in *Saints Are Now*

Read the stories of saints from various religious traditions. Identify the qualities of soul to look for in the saints of our times.

Celebrate

Celebration is a kind of food we all need in our lives, and each individual brings a special recipe or offering, so that together we will make a great feast. Celebration is a human need that we must not, and cannot deny. It is richer and fuller when many work and then celebrate together.

—CORITA KENT
and JAN STEWARD
in *Learning by Heart*

*Get together with friends
or family and celebrate one unique
thing about the day.*

Be Moderate

When you eat too much,
you forget your truth,

and fasting makes you conceited,
so eat with *some* discipline,
and consciously. Be
an ordinary human being.

Then the door will open,
and you'll recognize the way.
Lalla, be moderate!

—LALLA
in *Naked Song*

*Consider the ways you act
extremely, and moderate one of your
excessive behaviors.*

Appreciate Yourself

Some shamanic traditions in parts of Africa and the Oceanic societies attend to health and well-being through what is called *cradling work,* a four-part practice in staying connected to the good, true, and beautiful aspects of one's nature. In cradling work we lie on our back and place both hands over our heart (in many cultures hands symbolize healing). Silently, we acknowledge the character qualities that we appreciate about ourselves, we acknowledge our strengths, we acknowledge the contributions that have been made and continue to be made, and we acknowledge the love given and the love received.

—ANGELES ARRIEN
  in *The Four Fold Way*

*Compose a list of statements
to use as self-affirmations in
challenging situations.*

Battle Your Demons

To battle a demon is to embrace it, to face it with clarity of vision and humility of the heart. To run from a demon is as effective as running from a rabid dog, for surely this only beckons the chase. Whatever we resist—persists. These demons, these parts of us that haunt us, torture us, and reduce us, are the agents of change. They throw down the gauntlet to the warrior within us to face them in a duel.

—STEPHANIE ERICSSON
in *Companion Through the Darkness*

*Imagine that you are shining a
flashlight in the face of your demons.
How do they react? Stand your ground,
and see what happens.*

Love Your Neighbor

Who is our neighbor: the Samaritan? the outcast? the enemy? Yes, yes, of course. But it is also the whale, the dolphin, and the rain forest. Our neighbor is the entire community of life, the entire universe. We must love it all as ourself.

—BRIAN PATRICK
  quoted in *Earthspirit*

*Have you expanded the circle
of your love over the past year? Where
and how could you do this?*

Reframe

There is an old story about a man who wrote to the department of agriculture in his state to find out how to cope with the crabgrass that was spoiling his lawn. The department responded with a number of suggestions. The man tried them all, but he could not completely eliminate the crabgrass. Exasperated, he wrote the department again, noting that every method they had suggested had failed. His yard was still riddled with crabgrass. He got back a short reply: "We suggest you learn to love it."

That is the art of reframing, redefining something so that it is no longer as problematic. It isn't the situation that is changed, of course; it is your perspective on the situation.

—ROBERT H. and JEANETTE C. LAUER
in *Watersheds*

*Examine an old and persistent
problem from a new angle.*

Enjoy Moments of Happiness

I've been thinking about happiness—how wrong it is ever to expect it to last or there to be a time of happiness. It's not that, it's a *moment* of happiness. Almost every day contains at least one moment of happiness.

—MAY SARTON
in *Endgame*

*In a small notebook, keep a list of
moments of happiness you experience.*

Believe in Miracles

Miracles result from our recognition that even the worst news is only a short story; the whole plot is an unfolding mystery. Be humble in your perpetual uncertainty.

—PAUL PEARSALL
in *Making Miracles*

Look at the miracles you have experienced or witnessed in the lives of others. How much about them could you just never explain?

Live with Obstacles

For a long time it had seemed to me that life was about to begin—real life. But there was always some obstacle in the way, something to be got through first, some unfinished business, time still to be served, a debt to be paid. Then life would begin. At last it dawned on me that these obstacles were my life.

—ALFRED D'SOUZA
quoted in *Seven Choices*

*Name the most persistent
obstacles in your life.*

Create Balance

The Amish love the Sunshine and Shadow quilt pattern. It shows two sides—the dark and light, spirit and form—and the challenge of bringing the two into a larger unity. It's not a choice between extremes: conformity or freedom, discipline or imagination, acceptance or doubt, humility or a raging ego. It's a balancing act that includes opposites.

—SUE BENDER
  in *Plain and Simple*

*Think about your attempts to
achieve balance in your life. What spiritual
practices have you found helpful?*

Take Good Care of Your Partner

Our partner is a flower. If we take care of her well, she will grow beautifully. If we take care of her poorly, she will wither. To help a flower grow well, we must understand her nature. How much water does she need? How much sunshine? We look deeply into ourselves to see our true nature, and we look into the other person to see her nature.

—THICH NHAT HANH
in *Touching Peace*

*Give someone you love
a gift, a word of encouragement,
or an embrace.*

Find a Soul Friend

A soul friend is someone with whom we can share our greatest joys and deepest fears, confess our worst sins and most persistent faults, clarify our highest hopes and perhaps most unarticulated dreams.

—EDWARD C. SELLNER
in *Wisdom of the Celtic Saints*

Share a secret with a soul friend.

Thank Someone

One of the noblest words in our language is grace, defined as "unearned blessing." We live by grace far more than by anything else. Accordingly, I find that the one thing which I want to put into practice in my own life is the conscious and deliberate habit of finding somebody to thank.

—ELTON TRUEBLOOD
  in *The Courage to Grow Old*

---

*Say thank you to someone
who least expects it from you.*

Always Ask Permission

Never take a leaf or move a pebble without asking permission. Always ask permission. That maintains the balance and teaches humility. That leaf you want to pluck could be far more important than the little purpose you have in mind. You don't know—so ask permission first.

-—DON JOSÉ MATSUWA
quoted in *Profiles in Wisdom*

*Reflect upon the rights of animals,
plants, and other inhabitants of the earth.
Join an organization to protect them.*

Have Reverence

The soul suffers when we lack reverence. We live in an age that understands respect—respect earned through achievement, power, or actions. We live in an age that understands rights, obligations, and sets of commitments. But we have difficulty experiencing reverence because it comes from a deeper place. Reverence requires an experience of "otherness," the "thou-ness" of that other who crosses our path.

—D. STEPHENSON BOND
in *Living Myth*

*Take the feeling of being awestruck
and deeply moved and transfer it to
something close to home.*

Never Forget You May Be a Messenger

We understand that ordinary people are messengers of the Most High. They go about their tasks in holy anonymity. Often, even unknown to themselves. Yet, if they had not been there, if they had not said what they said or did what they did, it would not be the way it is now. We would not be the way we are now. Never forget that you too yourself may be a messenger.

—LAWRENCE KUSHNER
in *Honey from the Rock*

*Think of an instance when someone
called you an angel. Who has been a messenger
of the Most High for you?*

Rest in the Grace
of the World

When despair for the world grows in me
and I wake in the night at the least sound
in fear of what my life and my children's lives
    may be,
I go and lie down where the wood drake
rests in his beauty on the water, and the great
    heron feeds.
I come into the peace of wild things
who do not tax their lives with forethought
of grief. I come into the presence of still water.
And I feel above me the day-blind stars
waiting with their light. For a time
I rest in the grace of the world, and am free.

    —WENDELL BERRY
      in *Openings*

Remember the times in your life
when nature has given you solace.

Look to the Growing Edge

Look well to the growing edge. . . . It is the extra breath from the exhausted lung, the one more thing to try when all else has failed, the upward reach of life when weariness closes in upon all endeavor. This is the basis of hope in moments of despair, the incentive to carry on when times are out of joint and men have lost their reason, the source of confidence when worlds crash and dreams whiten into ash.

—HOWARD THURMAN
  in *For the Inward Journey*

*Name one person who has devoted
all of his or her energies to service or to a cause.
Try to follow his or her example.*

Kiss the Ground

Today, like every other day, we wake up empty
and frightened. Don't open the door to the study
and begin reading. Take down the dulcimer.
Let the beauty we love be what we do.
There are hundreds of ways to kneel and kiss the
    ground.

—RUMI
    in *Open Secret*

*Discover a new way
to embrace beauty and connect
with the sacred today.*

Groom Your Curiosity

The great affair, the love affair with life, is to live as variously as possible, to groom one's curiosity like a high-spirited thoroughbred, climb aboard, and gallop over the thick, sunstruck hills every day. . . . It began as mystery, and it will end in mystery, but what a savage and beautiful country lies in between.

—DIANE ACKERMAN
in *A Natural History of the Senses*

*Design a workout to keep
your curiosity fit. What exercises
would you include?*

Listen to Your Life

Listen to your life. See it for the fathomless mystery that it is. In the boredom and pain of it no less than in the excitement and gladness: touch, taste, smell your way to the holy and hidden heart of it because in the last analysis all moments are key moments, and life itself is grace.

—FREDERICK BUECHNER
   in *Now and Then*

*Surround yourself with the resources
that help you understand the spiritual
dimensions of your life experiences.
Be grateful to their creators.*

Come to the End of Words

Nothing less than the undivided universe can be our true home. Yet how can one speak or even think about the whole of things? Language is of only modest help. Every sentence is a wispy net, capturing a few flecks of meaning. The sun shines without vocabulary. The salmon has no name for the urge that drives it upstream. The newborn groping for the nipple knows hunger long before it knows a single word. Even with an entire dictionary in one's head, one eventually comes to the end of words. Then what? Then drink deep like the baby, swim like the salmon, burn like any brief star.

—SCOTT RUSSELL SANDERS
   in *Staying Put*

Take a deep breath and be silent.

Credits and Sources

Grateful acknowledgment is made for permission to reprint the following material:

1. Helen Mellicost. Quoted in *One Hundred Graces,* selected by Marcia and Jack Kelly. New York: Bell Tower, 1992.

2. Brief quotation from *A House with Four Rooms* by Rumer Godden. Copyright © 1989 by Rumer Godden. Reprinted by permission of William Morrow & Company, Inc.

3. Excerpt from p. 170 of *The Clown in the Belfry: Writings on Faith and Fiction* by Frederick Buechner. Copyright © 1992 by Frederick Buechner. Reprinted by permission of HarperCollins Publishers, Inc.

4. John Updike. Quoted in "Can a Nice Novelist Finish First?" (interview by Jane Howard). *Life* magazine, November 4, 1966.

5. Lawrence Kushner in *God Was in This Place and I, i Did Not Know: Finding Self, Spirituality and Ultimate Meaning.* Woodstock, VT: Jewish Lights Publishing, 1991 (p. 25). Permission granted by Jewish Lights Publishing, P.O. Box 237, Woodstock, VT 05091.

6. Abraham H. Maslow in *Religions, Values, and Peak-Experiences.* New York: Viking Press, 1972. Copyright © 1964 by Kappa Delta Pi, an International Honor Society in Education.

7. Excerpt from p. 287 of *Care of the Soul: A Guide for Cultivating Depth and Sacredness in Everyday Life* by Thomas Moore. Copyright © 1992 by Thomas Moore. Reprinted by permission of HarperCollins Publishers, Inc.

8. Alice O. Howell in *The Dove in the Stone: Finding the Sacred in the Commonplace.* Wheaton, IL: Quest Books, 1988.

9. Excerpted from *Touching Peace: Practicing the Art of Mindful Living* (1992) by Thich Nhat Hanh. Used with the permission of Parallax Press, Berkeley, CA.

10. Hasidic tale. Quoted in *Peacemaking Day by Day.* Erie, PA: Pax Christi, 1985.

11. Excerpt from p. 13 of *Choices (Making Right Decisions in a Complex World)* by Lewis B. Smedes. Copyright © 1986 by Lewis B. Smedes. Reprinted by permission of HarperCollins Publishers, Inc.

12. From *The More We Find in Each Other: Meditations for Couples* by Mavis and Merle Fossom. Copyright © 1992 by Hazelden Foundation, Center City, MN. Reprinted by permission.

13. H. L. Puxley in "The Church and the Paranormal." *International Journal of Parapsychology* 8, 2 (Spring 1966).

14. From *Money and the Meaning of Life* by Jacob Needleman. Copyright © 1991 by Jacob Needleman. Used by permission of Doubleday, a division of Bantam Doubleday Dell Publishing Group, Inc.

15. John of Ruysbroeck. Quoted in *The Common Experience: Signposts on the Path to Enlightenment* by J. M. Cohen and J.-F. Phipps. Wheaton, IL: Quest Books, 1992.

16. Shunryu Suzuki-roshi in *Zen Mind, Beginner's Mind*. New York: Weatherhill, 1970.

17. Brief quotation from *Family Tales, Family Wisdom: How to Gather the Stories of a Lifetime and Share Them with Your Family* by Dr. Robert U. Akeret with Daniel Klein. Copyright © 1991 by Robert Akeret and Daniel Klein. Reprinted by permission of William Morrow & Company, Inc.

18. Albert Schweitzer. Quoted in *The Search for Meaning: Americans Talk About What They Believe and Why* by Phillip L. Berman. Copyright © 1990 by Phillip L. Berman. New York: Ballantine, 1993.

19. David A. Cooper in *Silence, Simplicity, and Solitude: A Guide for Spiritual Retreat*. Copyright © 1992 by David Cooper. New York: Bell Tower, 1992.

20. Ram Dass in *Compassion in Action: Setting Out on the Path of Service* by Ram Dass and Mirabai Bush. Copyright © 1992 by Ram Dass and Mirabai Bush. New York: Bell Tower, 1992.

21. Robert C. Solomon in *A Passion for Justice: Emotions and the Origins of the Social Contract*. Copyright © 1990 by Robert C. Solomon. Reprinted by permission of Addison-Wesley Publishing Co., Inc., Reading, MA.

22. From *The Return of the Prodigal Son: A Meditation on Fathers, Brothers, and Sons* by Henri J. M. Nouwen. Copyright © 1992 by Henri J. M. Nouwen. Used by permission of Doubleday, a division of Bantam Doubleday Dell Publishing Group, Inc.

23. Excerpt from pp. 130–131 of *Wisdom Distilled from the Daily: Living the Rule of St. Benedict Today* by Joan D. Chittister. Copyright © 1990 by Joan D. Chittister. Reprinted by permission of HarperCollins Publishers, Inc.

24. *Simplicity: The Art of Living* by Richard Rohr. New York: Crossroad, 1993. Used by permission of The Crossroad Publishing Company.

25. Baal Shem Tov.

26. Lao Tzu. Quoted in *The Tao of Peace* by Diane Dreher. New York: Donald I. Fine, 1990 (p. 81). Reprinted by permission of Donald I. Fine, Inc.

27. "Karma Repair Kit: Items 1–4" from *The Pill Versus the Springhill Mine Disaster*. Copyright © 1968 by Richard Brautigan. Reprinted by permission of Houghton Mifflin Company. All rights reserved.

28. Barry Lopez in *The Rediscovery of North America.* Copyright © 1992 by Barry Lopez. Reprinted by permission of Sterling Lord Literistic, Inc.

29. Thomas Merton in *Contemplation in a World of Action*. Garden City, NY: Doubleday & Co., 1971 (p. 345).

30. Nancy Mellon in *Storytelling & the Art of Imagination*. Rockport, MA: Element, 1992 (p. 8).

31. Michael Grosso in *Soulmaker: True Stories from the Far Side of the Psyche*. Norfolk, VA: Hampton Roads Publishing, 1992 (p. 19).

32. Excerpt from *Pilgrim at Tinker Creek* by Annie Dillard. Copyright © 1974 by Annie Dillard. Reprinted by permission of HarperCollins Publishers, Inc.

33. Excerpt from p. 48 of *Creation Spirituality: Liberating Gifts for the Peoples of the Earth* by Matthew Fox. Copyright © 1991 by Matthew Fox. Reprinted by permission of HarperCollins Publishers, Inc.

34. From *Bill Moyers: A World of Ideas* by Bill Moyers. Copyright © 1989 by Public Affairs Television, Inc. Used by permission of Doubleday, a division of Bantam Doubleday Dell Publishing Group, Inc.

35. From *The Heart of the Enlightened* by Anthony de Mello, S. J. Copyright © 1989 by The Center for Spiritual Exchange. Used by permission of Doubleday, a division of Bantam Doubleday Dell Publishing Group, Inc.

36. Excerpt from p. 19 of *The Search for Signs of Intelligent Life in the Universe* by Jane Wagner. Copyright © 1986 by Jane Wagner Inc. Reprinted by permission of HarperCollins Publishers, Inc.

37. Excerpt from p. 18 of *A Joseph Campbell Companion: Reflections on the Art of Living*. Selected and edited by Diane K. Osbon. Copyright © 1991 by The Joseph Campbell Foundation. Reprinted by permission of HarperCollins Publishers, Inc.

38. From *The Blessings of Imperfection*, by G. Peter Fleck. Copyright © 1987 by G. Peter Fleck. Reprinted by permission of Beacon Press.

39. Rumi in *Unseen Rain, Quatrains of Rumi*. Translated by John Moyne and Coleman Barks. Putney, VT: Threshold Books, 1986. Reprinted by permission of Threshold Books, RD 4, Box 600, Putney, VT 05346.

40. From *Maybe (Maybe Not): Second Thoughts from a Secret Life* by Robert Fulghum. Copyright © 1993 by Robert Fulghum. Reprinted by permission of Villard Books, a division of Random House, Inc.

41. Excerpt from p. 253 of *The Passionate Life: Stages of Loving* by Sam Keen. Copyright © 1983 by Sam Keen. Reprinted by permission of HarperCollins Publishers, Inc.

42. From "Carnival" from *Soliloquies in England and Later Soliloquies* by George Santayana. Copyright © 1922. New York: Charles Scribner's Sons, 1922. Reprinted by permission of MIT Press.

43. Excerpt from p. 4 of *Rituals for Our Times: Celebrating, Healing, and Changing Our Lives and Our Relationships* by Evan Imber-Black and Janine

Roberts. Copyright © 1993 by Evan Imber-Black and Janine Roberts. Reprinted by permission of HarperCollins Publishers, Inc.

44. Excerpt from p. 186 of *Wisdom Distilled from the Daily: Living the Rule of St. Benedict Today* by Joan D. Chittister. Copyright © 1990 by Joan D. Chittister. Reprinted by permission of HarperCollins Publishers, Inc.

45. Joyce Rupp in *May I Have This Dance?* Notre Dame, IN: Ave Maria Press, 1992 (p. 118).

46. Valentin Tomberg in *Covenant of the Heart: Meditations of a Christian Hermeticist on the Mysteries of Tradition.* Rockport, MA: Element, 1992 (p. 78).

47. From *Hearts That We Broke Long Ago* by Merle Shain. Copyright © 1983 by The Estate of Merle Shain. Used by permission of Bantam Books, a division of Bantam Doubleday Dell Publishing Group, Inc.

48. From *Enjoying the World: The Rediscovery of Thomas Traherne* by Graham Dowell. Copyright © 1990. Used by permission of Morehouse Publishing.

49. From *Awareness* by Anthony de Mello, S.J., and J. Francis Stroud, S.J., editor. Copyright © 1990 by The Center for Spiritual Exchange. Used by permission of Doubleday, a division of Bantam Doubleday Dell Publishing Group, Inc.

50. From *The Wisdom of Heschel* (excerpt from "Wonder . . . Radical . . . Amazement . . . Awe") by Abraham Joshua Heschel. Edited by Ruth Marcus Goodhill. New York: Farrar, Straus & Giroux, 1975.

51. Helen M. Luke in *Kaleidoscope: "The Way of Woman" and Other Essays.* New York: Parabola Books, 1992 (p. 212).

52. Joseph Gosse in "Inexhaustible Springs." *Spiritual Life* 36, 1 (Spring 1990).

53. From *Learning by Heart* by Jan Steward and Corita Kent. Copyright © 1992 by Corita Kent and Jan Steward. Reprinted with permission from the Corita Art Center, Immaculate Heart Community.

54. Excerpt from p. 197 of *Apology for Wonder* by Sam Keen. Copyright © 1969 by Sam Keen. Reprinted by permission of HarperCollins Publishers, Inc.

55. Excerpt from p. 121 of *A Pretty Good Person* by Lewis B. Smedes. Copyright © 1990 by Lewis B. Smedes. Reprinted by permission of HarperCollins Publishers, Inc.

56. Brief quotation from *No Place Like Home: Rooms and Reflections from One Family's Life* by Linda Weltner. Copyright © 1988 by Linda Weltner. Reprinted by permission of William Morrow & Company, Inc.

57. David J. Wolpe in *In Speech and in Silence: The Jewish Quest for God.* New York: Henry Holt and Company. Copyright © 1992 by David J. Wolpe.

58. From *The Sabbath: Its Meaning for Modern Man* (excerpt from

p. 31 of "Beyond Civilization") by Abraham Joshua Heschel. Copyright © 1951 by Abraham Joshua Heschel. New York: Noonday, 1975.

59. *On Being a Friend* by Eugene Kennedy. Copyright © 1982 by Eugene Kennedy. Reprinted by permission of The Continuum Publishing Company.

60. Edward C. Sellner in *Mentoring: The Ministry of Spiritual Kinship.* Notre Dame, IN: Ave Maria Press, 1990 (p. 145).

61. Joanna Macy in *The Way Ahead: A Visionary Perspective for the New Millennium.* Edited by Eddie and Debbie Shapiro. Rockport, MA: Element, 1992 (p. 61).

62. Excerpt from p. 66 of *A Return to Love: Reflections on the Principles of A Course in Miracles* by Marianne Williamson. Copyright © 1992 by Marianne Williamson. Reprinted by permission of HarperCollins Publishers, Inc.

63. *Stripping Down: The Art of Spiritual Restoration* by Donna Schaper. Copyright © 1991 by LuraMedia, Inc., San Diego, CA.

64. John Welwood in *Ordinary Magic: Everyday Life as Spiritual Path.* Boston: Shambhala, 1992 (p. xiii).

65. Marion Woodman in an interview with China Galland (Rachel V.). Reprinted in *Conscious Femininity.* Toronto, Canada: Inner City Books, 1993 (pp. 44–45). Used by permission of China Galland.

66. From *The Alchemy of Illness* by Kat Duff. Copyright © 1993 by Kat Duff. Reprinted by permission of Pantheon Books, a division of Random House, Inc.

67. Excerpt from p. 48 of *Creation Spirituality: Liberating Gifts for the Peoples of the Earth* by Matthew Fox. Copyright © 1991 by Matthew Fox. Reprinted by permission of HarperCollins Publishers, Inc.

68. Michael Crichton in *Travels.* Copyright © 1988 by Michael Crichton. New York: Alfred A. Knopf, 1988.

69. Thomas Bender in *The Power of Place: Sacred Ground in Natural & Human Environments.* Edited by James A. Swan. Wheaton, IL: Quest Books, 1991.

70. Clarissa Pinkola Estés in *Women Who Run with the Wolves: Myths and Stories of the Wild Woman Archetype.* Copyright © 1992 by Clarissa Pinkola Estés. New York: Ballantine, 1992.

71. Excerpt from p. 304 of *Care of the Soul: A Guide for Cultivating Depth and Sacredness in Everyday Life* by Thomas Moore. Copyright © 1992 by Thomas Moore. Reprinted by permission of HarperCollins Publishers, Inc.

72. Excerpted from *Letters to My Son* by Kent Nerburn, 1993. Reprinted with permission of New World Library, San Rafael, CA 94903.

73. Brief quotation from *No Place Like Home: Rooms and Reflections from One Family's Life* by Linda Weltner. Copyright © 1988 by Linda Weltner. Reprinted by permission of William Morrow & Company, Inc.

74. *Healthy Pleasures* (pp. 200–201), copyright © 1990 by Robert Ornstein, Ph.D., and David Sobel, M.D. Reprinted by permission of Perseus Books Publishers, a member of Perseus Books, L.L.C.

75. From *The Book of Embraces* ("Art and Time," p. 244) by Eduardo Galeano. Translated by Cedric Belfrage with Mark Schafer. New York: W. W. Norton, 1992.

76. The Talmud. Quoted in *Storytelling & the Art of Imagination* by Nancy Mellon. Rockport, MA: Element, 1992.

77. From *Maybe (Maybe Not): Second Thoughts from a Secret Life* by Robert Fulghum. Copyright © 1993 by Robert Fulghum. Reprinted by permission of Villard Books, a division of Random House, Inc.

78. From *Saints Are Now* by John J. Delaney. Copyright © 1981 by John J. Delaney. Used by permission of Doubleday, a division of Bantam Doubleday Dell Publishing Group, Inc.

79. From *Learning by Heart* by Jan Steward and Corita Kent. Copyright © 1992 by Corita Kent and Jan Steward. Reprinted with permission from the Corita Art Center, Immaculate Heart Community.

80. Lalla. *Naked Song.* Translated by Coleman Barks. Athens, GA: Maypop Books, 1992. Reprinted by permission of Maypop Books, 196 Westview Dr., Athens, GA 30606.

81. Excerpt from pp. 61–62 of *The Four-Fold Way: Walking the Paths of the Warrior, Teacher, Healer, and Visionary* by Angeles Arrien. Copyright © 1993 by Angeles Arrien. Reprinted by permission of HarperCollins Publishers, Inc.

82. Excerpt from pp. 53–54 of *Companion Through the Darkness: Inner Dialogues on Grief* by Stephanie Ericsson. Copyright © 1993 by Stephanie Ericsson. Reprinted by permission of HarperCollins Publishers, Inc.

83. Brian Patrick. Quoted in *Earthspirit: A Handbook for Nurturing an Ecological Unity* by Michael Dowd. Mystic, CT: Twenty-Third Publications, 1991. Reprinted by permission of Twenty-Third Publications, P.O. Box 180, Mystic, CT 06355.

84. From *Watersheds: Mastering Life's Unpredictable Crises* by Robert H. Lauer, Ph.D., and Jeanette C. Lauer, Ph.D. Copyright © 1988 by Robert H. Lauer, Ph.D., and Jeanette C. Lauer, Ph.D. By permission of Little, Brown and Company.

85. From *Endgame: A Journal of the Seventy-ninth Year* by May Sarton. New York: W. W. Norton, 1992 (p. 250).

86. From *Making Miracles* by Paul Pearsall, Ph.D. Copyright © 1991. Reprinted with the permission of Simon & Schuster, Inc.

87. Alfred D'Souza. Quoted in *Seven Choices: Taking the Steps to New Life After Losing Someone You Love* by Elizabeth Harper Neeld. Copyright © 1990 by Neeld & Neeld, Inc. New York: Clarkson N. Potter, Inc., 1990.

88. Excerpt from p. 146 of *Plain and Simple: A Woman's Journey to the*

Amish by Sue Bender. Copyright © 1991 by Sue Bender. Reprinted by permission of HarperCollins Publishers, Inc.

89. Excerpted from *Touching Peace: Practicing the Art of Mindful Living* (1992) by Thich Nhat Hanh. Used with permission of Parallax Press, Berkeley, CA.

90. Edward C. Sellner in *Wisdom of the Celtic Saints*. Notre Dame, IN: Ave Maria Press, 1993 (p. 8).

91. Elton Trueblood in *The Courage to Grow Old*. Edited by Phillip L. Berman. New York: Ballantine, 1989.

92. Don José Matsuwa. Reprinted from *Profiles in Wisdom: Native Elders Speak About the Earth* by Steve McFadden. Copyright © 1991, Bear & Company, P.O. Box 2860, Santa Fe, NM 87504.

93. D. Stephenson Bond in *Living Myth: Personal Meaning as a Way of Life*. Boston: Shambhala, 1993 (p. 177).

94. Lawrence Kushner in *Honey from the Rock: Visions of Jewish Mystical Renewal*. Woodstock, VT: Jewish Lights, 1990. Permission granted by Jewish Lights Publishing, P.O. Box 237, Woodstock, VT 05091.

95. "The Peace of Wild Things" from *Openings*. Copyright © 1968 by Wendell Berry. Reprinted by permission of the author.

96. Excerpt from *For the Inward Journey: The Writings of Howard Thurman* by Anne Spencer Thurman. Copyright © 1984 by Sue Bailey Thurman. Reprinted by permission of Harcourt Brace & Company.

97. Rumi in *Open Secret: Versions of Rumi*. Translated by John Moyne and Coleman Barks. Putney, VT: Threshold Books, 1984. Reprinted by permission of Threshold Books, RD 4, Box 600, Putney, VT 05346.

98. Diane Ackerman in *A Natural History of the Senses*. Copyright © 1990 by Diane Ackerman. New York: Random House, 1990.

99. Excerpt from p. 87 of *Now and Then* by Frederick Buechner. Copyright © 1983 by Frederick Buechner. Reprinted by permission of HarperCollins Publishers, Inc.

100. From *Staying Put: Making a Home in a Restless World* by Scott Russell Sanders. Copyright © 1993 by Scott Russell Sanders. Reprinted by permission of Beacon Press.

About the Editors

Frederic and Mary Ann Brussat have been covering contemporary culture and spiritual renaissance for three decades. They wrote the magazine *Values & Visions: A Resource Companion for Spiritual Journeys,* which Bill Moyers called "the most original and refreshing guide to what's truly valuable in American society." The Brussats are continuing this kind of positive reviewing of new books, spoken-word audios, feature films, and videos for other religious and spiritual publications, including *Spirituality & Health* and *The Lutheran.* They also have developed some 250 *Values & Visions* discussion guides for small groups interested in using books and movies as catalysts to soulmaking.

Mary Ann and Frederic are the authors of *Spiritual Literacy: Reading the Sacred in Everyday Life,* a collection of more than 600 examples of spiritual perspectives on everyday experience, which as been made into a 26-week television series. In a companion book, *Spiritual Rx: Prescriptions for a Meaningful Life,* they recommend the best ways to explore 37 spiritual practices that are common in the world religions.

Readers can find information on the Brussats' books, discussion guides, and other projects on their web site at www.valuesandvisions.org. New recommendations of spiritual resources are posted every week, and a database contains thousands of recent reviews. Readers can also sign up to receive free e-mail "Soul Boosters" containing quotes and practice suggestions in the format the Brussats pioneered in *100 Ways to Keep Your Soul Alive* and its sequel, *100 More Ways to Keep Your Soul Alive.*

Frederic is a United Church of Christ clergyman with a journalism ministry. The Brussats live in New York City.

For more information on the Brussats' work and publications, visit www.valuesandvisions.org or write: Values & Visions, P.O. Box 786, Dept. 100H, Madison Square Station, New York, NY 10159.